# MY FAVORITE WARLORD

# MY FAVORITE WARLORD

EUGENE GLORIA

PENGUIN POETS

PENGUIN BOOKS
Published by the Penguin Group
Penguin Group (USA) Inc., 375 Hudson Street,
New York, New York 10014, U.S.A.
Penguin Group (Canada), 90 Eglinton Avenue East, Suite 700,
Toronto, Ontario, Canada M4P 2Y3 (a division of Pearson Penguin Canada Inc.)
Penguin Books Ltd, 80 Strand, London WC2R 0RL, England
Penguin Ireland, 25 St Stephen's Green, Dublin 2,
Ireland (a division of Penguin Books Ltd)
Penguin Group (Australia), 250 Camberwell Road, Camberwell,
Victoria 3124, Australia (a division of Pearson Australia Group Pty Ltd)
Penguin Books India Pvt Ltd, 11 Community Centre, Panchsheel Park,
New Delhi – 110 017, India
Penguin Group (NZ), 67 Apollo Drive, Rosedale, Auckland 0632,
New Zealand (a division of Pearson New Zealand Ltd)
Penguin Books (South Africa) (Pty) Ltd, 24 Sturdee Avenue,
Rosebank, Johannesburg 2196, South Africa

Penguin Books Ltd, Registered Offices:
80 Strand, London WC2R 0RL, England

First published in Penguin Books 2012

1   3   5   7   9   10   8   6   4   2

Copyright © Eugene Gloria, 2012
All rights reserved

Pages 75 and 76 constitute an extension of this copyright page.

LIBRARY OF CONGRESS CATALOGING IN PUBLICATION DATA
Gloria, Eugene.
My favorite warlord / Eugene Gloria.
p. cm.—(Penguin poets)
Poems.
ISBN 978-0-14-312140-4
I. Title.
PS3557.L6485M9 2012
811'.54—dc23
2012004340

Printed in the United States of America
Set in Bembo
Designed by Ginger Legato

ALWAYS LEARNING                                                    PEARSON

*For my mother and father*

# CONTENTS

**PART 3**

**PART 4**

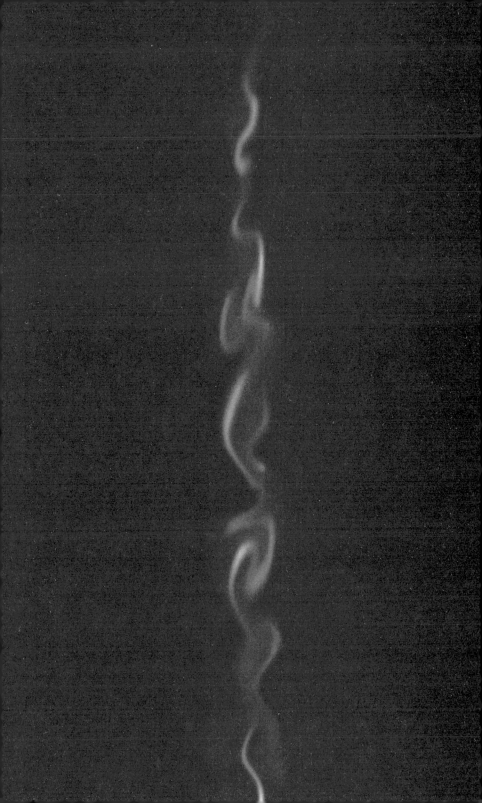

# MY FAVORITE WARLORD

# PART 1

## ■ WATER

The street when I was five
was a deep, wide river
coursing through a shimmering city.
I had no need for proper shoes,
no need for long pants.
I didn't yet know how to make
conclusions and say, "Life's like this . . ."

You could say I was baptized by a red circle
at the center of my forehead—a constellation

of tiny scabs, federated by Mercurochrome.
Why the dots on my forehead?
                And why, you might ask,
did I want to cross the glistening street?
I had crossed my brother and in his anger
he chucked the whiskbroom; its edge-tip
handle smacked my forehead.
I was five, my brother was fifteen.

What was he doing washing his body
at the spigot behind the house?

I caught him bathing
not in the shower where he should've been,
but alone in the small yard, a tin
can in his hand, dousing his head with water.
Why did I laugh when I saw him?

What did I know about anything?
Was this the beginning
of my brother's rage? Was this the birth

of water? The cool drink
an old woman wanted and I, instead of

directing her to the kitchen where
a pitcher of water was chilling in the icebox,
led her to the spigot out back.
There is no story here. No melody
to this song; only a street and what
punishment metes to the one who wants
what he knows he cannot have.
                    And the water?

The whole expanse of it—
was only a street I wanted to cross.

Imagine the pleasure inside this storm,
the foam rush from rain gutters. Imagine
yourself here, inside a restaurant

on an unlit street. Say it is a bad neighborhood
even after the rain. Take the immigrant face
of our waiter who is also the proprietor. Say:

Peter, it's been weeks. We've come to eat.
We've been hankering for your *pho*.
We know what we want—

the same meal we always order—
me, the no. 1 appetizer; my wife, the no. 3.
For our entrées, the no. 38 and the no. 30.

The booths here are lit by bright faces:
Vietnamese, Thai, Chinese, and Filipino.
Hundreds of years on their faces!

Schoolteachers, witnesses of terror, readers
of Chekhov, office clerks with inner lives.
Then the bottle-blond salaryman

in a dress shirt with silver cuff links
moseys in to pick up his takeout order.
He is tall and pockmarked

like my father; he could almost be
my father except for the dyed blond hair.
Over the no. 1 and no. 3 appetizers,

we are speculating, my wife and I,
where the salaryman comes from—
Manila or Saigon?

Oh, but here comes Peter with our orders
of steaming bowls of *pho*. Our faces
shining like klieg lights.

Inside this booth, my moon face
is a lantern in the mainstream
lengthening, lengthening.

Here, on earth we are curtained by rain.
A subset in the far corners floating
toward the center. We are an island

in landlocked America. We are
Thai, Filipino, and Vietnamese.
We are, all of us, post exotics.

## ■ APPLE

My people are never the same in memory.
They are the dead come back for a picnic,
a table set with plates of sliced apples.
I am there somewhere hidden in a tree.
In my luckless twenties, still raw from heart-
break and prone to constant hard-ons, I watched
through an open window a woman, middle-aged,
naked except for her utilitarian bra and panties.
Her hair teased like a hive of cotton candy,
eyelids a heavy purple coat. I could almost
smell her—vivid as my first kiss: Maile L.
who had in her mouth some cinnamon Red Hots.
The woman's lipstick was thick like car wax
red and cheap in a dime-store way.
She was fixing to go to work at some diner.
I was then a college intern for the lame duck
from my district. I was eager for everything
I imagined this woman could teach me.
This was in the city of Cain where we kept
the doors unlocked for alien thoughts to enter.
If she were the first woman, would that make
me the snake? See, the snake in the garden
was a real smoothy with a killer pickup line.
Me, I was just a salamander on a leaf.
This, before I learned my left from my right,

Rilke from Roethke, Keats from Yeats.
And many more years followed when I didn't
understand a thing completely. Memory
is another name for ghosts and their awful hunger.

The moon is the mind of Buddha.
The rabbit in the moon is a story.
Says so here in my book.

My book is the necessary nothing
celebrating the fortieth anniversary
of a nonevent. In the free market
there are maxims to live by:

*The consumer isn't a moron.*
*She is your wife.* In the gift economy
a trellis of vines is a splendid thing.
Walk under it, et cetera.

Who am I to tell you my story when I am no taller than the trees
or hills or other humans? That I am as tenuous as our rabbit sleep-
ing away his days; that he and I are frail leaves floating along the
same river. What was it Whitman meant when he said, "I believe
a leaf of grass is no less than the journeywork of the stars"? Forty
years ago in the middle of June, a flood of white light bathed an
airport runway. Forty years ago, the moon still awaited its birth.
*What was there at the beginning? Was there a beginning?* When the
rabbit met the Buddha, the rabbit made a fire and tried to gather
some food. Finding none, the rabbit offered itself to the Buddha
by jumping into the fire. Freighted memory, refugee city, we
landed and then the taxi driver dropped our luggage on the curb.
And here, now in the middle of America, I can only imagine the
figures huddled in the fog, their slight and foreign bodies.

The shut-in nuns had prayed for sun
and the long blue sky, a time
when my father was called Isidro.
Whatever story I tell about him
is incomplete unless I first tell you
this one: I was seven that monsoon season
before the highway had a proper name,
before my father became a U.S. citizen
and shortened his name to Sid.
He took me to a convent on Highway 54.

"Women there," he said, "hide their faces from the world."
The convent had a narrow hallway, which wound
around an austere chapel scented with jasmine.
A paneled door opened with a squeak; a cupboard
kept, instead of plates and cups, a partition of wire mesh.

A voice—no, a whisper—filtered through.
I had to stand on tiptoes to see whose mouth that was—
an outline of a face. A voice unused to conversation:
"Please," she said in a halting dialect I didn't know,
"leave your offering at the front pew
and may God . . . grant you . . . both . . . safe travels."
The mesh screen darkened and then
the paneled door slid shut.
We brought three dozen eggs plus four
and did with them what the voice instructed.

Later that day, there was a long procession
from the old church to what seemed then
a widening street where my father led
a company of men with his sword drawn,
resting on one shoulder. He was in full feather:
tippet, pleated shirt, bow tie, shiny lapels, cloak.
He wore the plumed hat of the Grand Knight.
And men dressed like him, who in daily life
were doctors, dentists like my godfather,
or minor officials, marched two by two toward
long tables where anyone who chose to celebrate
could come and eat. There were no homeless
in our town, no one was starving. Everyone had food
in their kitchens with maids to tend to them.
Therefore, the feast had more to do with coming
together and how important it was to do so.

There was eating and drinking till night.
And because of the eggs we brought earlier that day,
the rain ceased for the better part of the week.

A chorus lifts above the mundane spaces:

                    Silences and asterisks of dust—

My urge to write about the new disasters,

               Homelands submerged, blasted

Coral reefs; a cask of dynamite

               Has lent its method on the page.

Facts can melt away abstractions. New names for receptacles,

               Jeweled palaces.

A ceremony of particulars: family portraits, a dance in fragments,

               Postcards, a rusted tin of SkyFlakes.

Designed to intrude as little as possible into tea drinking, this bowl has the appearance of weightiness. Fired at low temperature and therefore less durable. Rustic and imperfect, the bowl seems to contradict preciousness. Fragile and suggestive, the Great Black assumes nothing but its own impermanence. For three generations this bowl for tea ceremony was passed down from fathers to sons, from one potter to another. Art inseparable from occupation is not an ambition but a way. I have lost my way in the process. Souls of no objects descended without warning. Listening to the *shi, shi, shi* of shoeless feet, middle-aged women in silk kimonos assembled in front of the glassed-in shelves of raku bowls and flower vases, a bouquet of pink and purple silk reflected on the glass.

# ■ PSALM FOR READING SKY

Starlings, slight as dew, and so many—
indices: Arabic, numeric, 1, 2, 3, you get me, man?
I'm longing for a brief season of snow ploughs

and orange belly dumps salting icy roads, of tulips
in their gayest skirts arriving like the implacable
grackles in their shiny coats and spectator shoes.

I need my bad old uncles who kiss for luck
and leave their wives in borrowed dresses.
I need them to school me on some bad intelligence

like landlords who torch their shacks for insurance
and squint at the pink clouds for want of starlings—
their inked ledgers running wet with gasoline.

I thought at first it was smoke from a fire in the hills—
but they fanned in and around, aimless flock
like the wreckage of commas splicing with abandon.

# ■ PSALM WITH LATHE AND KNIFE

At eight a.m. still dark, intrepid businesses: tellers
counting their tills, a mechanic lighting up
his lube bay, dust, decorum, nest of bees,

fireflies, albumen splatter, comb, fan,
umbrella, lathe, knife, bees of appropriation,
objects of the late world.

An ocean is the sound of tires on rain-swept asphalt.
Home is a road of trailer parks on one end,
an auto parts factory on the other.

Out of the back lots of ruin rises
a resilient island. It is a town called the present
where my headlights are tunneling north.

# ■ A NET OF CLOUDS IS WHAT WE FLOAT

A net of clouds is what we float
on a string and call our father.
Memory and forgetting,
two versions of the same story.

Fill in the holes, spackle the cracks,
and don't forget about the hay.
Old bale of hay stored in a plastic bin
big enough to hide a human body.

When I pulled open the bin
a pungent odor of tobacco assailed us
like regret. All shapes and shades
of memory seized my wife and me.

*Kulimlim*, inauspicious clouds,
*kulambo*, a mosquito net we string,
float over sleep mats in the provinces,
farther father, further memory goes.

We continued sweeping and clearing out
the stuff kept for our rabbits.
Now that Girlie is no longer with us,
the last of our two pets to move on,

it's time to throw away the hay bale,
clear a space for the pedestal sink, cast-
iron tub, and matching stool arriving
via Amtrak then a semi driven by Mike,

or Stan from Wichita with his brand-new
Class 1 license and air brake permit.
And the scent of tobacco from the bin
is not what I would associate with change

though for now a cosmic precursor
to the Tri-County Builders,
longtime Jehovah's Witnesses,
and tobacco-smoking dungaree types.

"So tell me," I query the more senior
of the two, "what is the color of memory?"
Maybe he will regard this interrogative
as a directive, dismissing all suspicion.

Let him answer me in the frivolous affirmative,
"Yes, I can build a gambrel over your grief,
order up a bas-relief, an encaustic tableau
of three birds, the color of cigarette stain."

# PART 2

*[japan  tr. v. 1. To decorate with a black enamel or lacquer.
2. To coat with a glossy finish.* American Heritage Dictionary*]*

A lacquer tray with matching bowls. None of which I have seen before with their bold lyric lines echoing rust and rough seas. *Think of the sea as weight. Think of the oar as a lever.* The maker of the lacquer tray with matching bowls would not call this art. There is no art in describing art just as there was no word for art until the old world became "the new." Take my brother's English, which is limited to an old idiom for the woman who shares his bed. My brother, who says "my wife" even when the referent is next to him and therefore distanced by the appellation, is now sixty and has warded off cussing almost entirely. His expletives have been replaced by a Disney-coated lingo. "Ah, Jiminy Cricket," he'd shout in frustration. "Dang it," an Indiana high schooler exclaimed to me at my door when I told her I'd already bought the local discount card she was hawking to benefit her school band. I mourn my brother's bygone expletives. They were so colorful, so native; his cussing, especially in Tagalog, had touches of tropical baroque. His maturity has given in to rhetorical silence, his private code of civility.

Silence, in Shibata Zeshin's craft, is artistic instead of rhetorical. Zeshin (1807–1891) was considered the genius of Japanese lacquer. He understood the delicate grain of Chinese rosewood. A wood-chip base and lacquer coat make for a durable bowl and serving tray. In Kyoto, Monju, a store run by a family making lacquerware for several generations, is where to find the best quality. In the old world, brides were given a set of boxwood combs kept in a beautiful lacquer box, combs passed down from mother to daughter and on down the line. My brother takes a break after a long day entertaining guests and slumps on the lounge chair in his family room, the TV on for company. My brother is at sea. Blue skies, calm waters. The only world he understands is the present. To understand my brother is to know the function of nature as a thing in perpetual labor of evolution. I pretend to know him. Look at my brother's face while he sleeps. Say he looks his age, a man lapping his sixties. At my wedding in Detroit ten years ago, he was proud as a peacock in his fitted suit, a gunmetal gray in a sea of white lace. The light of his being is now dimmed to a 20-watt bulb. He looks like our father, whose evolutionary snapshot was the Peking man—skull of a man in a perpetual grin. Sometimes your gaze can burn a hole right through the object you are looking at—say like prose affording us the lapidary focus in contrast to the lyric's tendency toward the blurred image. As one learns to add and subtract pure, disembodied emotion, life unlike lacquer will always be rounded by death.

Diane Arbus is studying a couple
looking at her photograph,
"Girl in a Shiny Dress."
She's reading the couple's faces,
the curl of the corner
of the woman's mouth, the knit
of her brow. She wants her to nod
in approval; no, she just wants
them to feel something and forget
where they are. But the man wears
a smirk, then remarks, "Even I
can take this picture." She plucks
out her pocket-size notebook,
flips to a fresh page, and scribbles
what he said. There is a war.
My oldest sister is still a virgin
and vaguely resembles the woman
in the photo "Girl in a Shiny Dress."
There is a war, and when
both sides decide to call it quits,
there will be a U.S. tally of 58,000 dead.
I am ten, bone-spare and formless,
mimicking a new dance. The exhibit's
theme is the "New Social Landscape."
In the Summer of Love
Diane Arbus prowls our street.
She buys a postcard in the Haight
and joins the antiwar movement.

She writes to a friend in London
about her show at the MoMA
and in her diary confesses
that she adores freaks. In her
Moleskine notebook, she records
another photograph of a man
right out of a Flannery O'Connor
story: a portrait of intensity,
a face fraught with good intentions.
"Boy with a Straw Hat Waiting
to March in a Pro-war Parade."
Around Christmas, "I Second
That Emotion" is the most popular
song on the radio, and Smokey
Robinson's porcelain voice testifies
to keep us where we were,
a sound telling us that he's
bitten into the moon's dark
flesh to hold the stars
in their place. And all of us stayed
put in our small but brilliant
constellation, managing to escape
unscathed from the camera's long gaze.

# ■ ALLEGORY OF THE LAUNDROMAT

Another Emilie Loring romance, her third in one month:
    "How could she hope that his love would remain
    steadfast when he learned her shameful secret?"

It was 1967 and the phenomenal world tethered on the brink
of laundry baskets and record snowfall in Chicago, astronauts burning
in their space capsule, Wole Soyinka being hauled to jail

on trumped-up charges, eighty-two arrests in a police raid at a blind pig
in Detroit precipitating a riot. "Here Comes the Night"
was what my sister heard the band rehearsing

on the rooftop three backyards away through a cloisonné
of clotheslines and pulleys. The hippie drummer waved
his drumsticks, my sister wishing for a Van Morrison song.

This was the year Che was ambushed,
the summer Fidel would seek refuge in Spanish Harlem
and pluck chickens on a neighbor's porch stoop, the year

my sister was almost raped at a Laundromat in the Haight.
It was Saturday in fog-banked San Francisco, my sister,
negotiating between delicates and perma press, between dark

and semidark socks with danger and romance.
There was no escaping that Magdalenic task of laundry,
loads upon nuanced loads she carted from our flat.

She was indentured not to nuns who took in troubled teens
from "good families," but to a mother at work on a weekend.
"When a Man Loves a Woman" played on a scratched 45

over and over from the tomboy's bedroom below our flat.
There was no escaping the oily man in a brown derby jacket
in that near-empty Laundromat that afternoon.

He came from behind and put his left hand across her mouth
and his other on her crotch just when she was about to read
Emilie Loring describe the waywardness of the heart

to the rhythm of the rinse cycle. "Here Comes the Night"
was not playing in her head, but the drummer
walked in on them and spooked her attacker.

The hippie drummer with his dopey Labrador
was on his way to the park . . . Vietnam, the Six-Day War,
black riots in Newark and Detroit, all that bedlam and rage,

and it was hotter than an immolating monk in July.
Who gives a hoot about the flood of runaways from Nebraska?
Who gives a whit about the indelicate balance of our weekly wash?

## ■ INTIMACY

Hiroshige must have understood proportion
in his print "Evening Squall at Ōhashi":
the smallness of men under a prodigious storm.

Night of folding umbrellas and a harvest
of shadows, I set out on foot
and ducked into the covered shopping arcade

on Teramachi and took my dinner
there at my favorite tonkatsu restaurant.
Rain kept pouring and singing in the gutters.

I remembered taking a shower
with two of my big sisters when they were still
part boy, hairless below with swoosh lines,

no breasts to speak of. I was but a twig
enclosed by the tan barks of madrones,
my young sisters towering over me,

and tonight I am wholly honored
by this intimate memory.
On BBC World I watched a news item

about a seventeen-year-old girl
dragged by the hair then kicked
and stoned to death by her brothers

for being with a man rumored to be her lover.
In Kurosawa's *Rashomon,* the thief
scoffs at the priest,

"If this is a sermon, I'd rather listen to the rain."
What punishment would you heap
upon my sisters who harbor such an intimacy?

It is raining in the ancient city,
so much rain! I am small in the rain.

## ■ ELEGY FOR ISHIKAWA GOEMON

The warlord Hideyoshi will do what he must
by the banks of the Kamogawa where Goemon
and his son will be boiled in oil. That night
Goemon consulted his ancestors. When daylight
came he realized that he had no wear of ore
being the son of the son of a thief.
Fog that morning assumed an armor of rust.
On the day of his capture, Ishikawa Goemon
began to see each grain of sand swirling in the air.
From the plane, a massif emerged below
like a rumpled army blanket. Hideyoshi was
fond of novel ideas and wore a surcoat,
woven in Persia with birds and beasts
embroidered in pretty colors.
One can see the bridge over Nagasaki Bay
from the cockpit. Sixty-four years ago,
heat rays from the bomb blast caused
various phenomena on the surface of objects.

## ■ NEW ZEALAND

In second grade, Sister Mary George
said that we live in the age of discovery—
and one day we'd land on the moon.

Ovals and Qs, letters linking into words
in their curvy shapes like the prow of a ship.
Two of my big sisters showed me how.

My sisters skipped rope with rhymes, sang,
"Magellan, MacArthur, and Lapu-Lapu."
At St. Agnes in the Haight, Sister Mary George

placed a letter in my hand. From New Zealand!
A pen pal, therefore, I became—even when
English was hard for me to speak—

to somebody's son in Auckland who signed
off with a sunny "cheers" and regaled
me with stories of his Uncle Bunny.

I also knew another boy, Jesse—
more from the scratches he made,
what looked like Greek

on his Big Chief notepad. Our world
was a pond where you could
skip a rock from end to end.

Waller Street was where Jesse and I lived.
My family rented a flat there, our first.
Shotgun hallways, vaulted ceilings,

a claw-foot tub, bay windows.
Janis Joplin shoring up supplies
from our corner Chinese grocer.

In class, Jesse sat at the very back.
Wendy Matsuo sat across the aisle from him.
Jad Nadal sniffled behind me.

Jad, who had a long upper torso and floppy ears,
was clueless to my constant stops
at the pencil sharpener by the cloakroom.

I copied his workbook. I was shameless.
Once, on my way to the sharpener,
I spied a curious thing: Jesse's hand

misplaced inside Wendy Matsuo's skirt.
Arms long, the cuff of his green sweater
well above the bone of his wrist.

On a tour, years later in my middle age,
I would gape at what's supposed to be
the wristbone of John the Baptist

encased in gold, studded with rubies,
in Topkapi Palace. I was there
with my wife. Never told her about

Jesse and his hand rambling
along the floral fields of Wendy's
panties, and Wendy all saintly—

her face a blank space we filled in
with the right words in our workbook.
In religion class Wendy said, "God

made all the flowers in the world
to show His love for us." How profound
this must have sounded to our nun—

Wendy her pet. Miss Brown Nose's twin.
Jesse had beautiful hands (imagine them encased
in gold, studded with rubies!)—

Jesse had a red Afro. He had light skin.
Hate is too harsh a word, but I must have said it
because of Wendy. Because I feared him.

Sister Mary George declared
the world was round,
though we knew this already.

This was the age of discovery!
And Sister Mary George, who'd made me
a pen pal, said she had proof.

It wasn't because of Magellan
(as I had known it from my sisters).
John Glenn, Sister said, sent photos

of Earth from his tiny ship—
waxy shapes of clouds, rain shadows
over Lake Taupo in the South Island,

Land of the Long White Cloud!
I don't think I was envious of Jesse
and the encumbrances of his discoveries,

nor did I ever take a shine to Wendy.
Her sorry familial traits: short legs,
flat nose, dark skin, her cloying obedience.

Jane Kelly was more my speed.
White with dark hair, Irish American,
and passably pretty. What does this make me?

By third grade the whole class
was writing in cursive—elongated ovals gliding
and uncoiling like helical springs.

My letters to the boy from New Zealand
ended as quickly as they began.
No more dreams of Māori longboats,

no more Uncle Bunny who hailed
from Auckland, and that kid Jesse
and his sisters would later transfer

to the public school. Back then we
still saw each other on Waller Street
until he, too, disappeared

into the white cloud hanging over
what must have looked like a pond
from John Glenn's tin-can ship.

Miles Davis is a barbiturate ride of non sequiturs: blue lines criss-crossing a subway map of Tokyo. When I was ten, all the slickers dripping in the cloakroom were yellow. A girl, one of the Mary Anns or Mary Catherines, had red rubber boots. My father wore a blue Ban-Lon shirt. Once, I watched my father get berated by his boss after I dropped him off at work. Pity the boss for his inconvenience; pity the father if you must for having a son who made him late. In my twenties, I heard Miles Davis blow his horn; his back was turned to the audience. This was a couple of years before he died. I was not old enough to understand his horn's conceit, or that

Miles Davis was an idea. "So What" began as a memory of his father. Then two cops came and busted his head open while he was taking a cigarette break outside the recording studio. Copping an attitude is a sure invitation for an ass-whuppin'. In front of a giant sequoia you learn to let go of your conceit. There is snow on the ground like remnants of an accident. In his holy writ, William Matthews proclaims: "Here it comes, Grief's beautiful blow job."

> Someone give my old man a sobriquet
> for his sense of timing, his miscues.
> Someone make him a song
> immediate and transparent!
> Let it be sung with trumpets—
> trouble's durable democracies.

# ■ THE 24-HOUR ASIAN AS A CULTURAL COMPETITOR

My kung fu is better than your kung fu.
My kung fu can pickpocket your heart,

cut you with a knifehand straight
to the scented herbage of your breast.

Your kung fu don't know sashimi
from a *shonen* knife, can't tell a hop-along coolie

from a fortune cookie caricature,
a *japayuki* from corn in Kansas.

Name is Fu and I got my ninja throwing stars
soaring toward your future.

I am your *Australopithecus* original,
your melancholy primitive. I am your de facto courage,
your Frank Sinatra fairy tale.

# ■ MY FAVORITE WARLORD

*"Hello, hello, hello . . . "*

—KURT COBAIN

I see him now on borrowed time, a big soft man in his pink T-shirt.
    This was my last image of my father: a stooped man

turning the faucet on to water his lawn. "Hello," I say in my heart,
    and then drive away, not waving. Men are cowards

compared to flowers. That much I know. In their solitude and beauty,
    flowers say, "I have sacrificed myself for you."

Just as the omuro blossoms in the temple have surrendered
    themselves to the wind. Unlike my father,

my favorite warlord is an irascible manager—suspicious
    of foreign intrigues and change. When the tea master

Rikyu leveled his prized garden of morning glories
    and replaced it with streams of sand

and sculpted mounds for moon-viewing, Hideyoshi was livid.
    "Hello, Hideyoshi, hello" were Rikyu's first words

as the warlord entered through the door. "Join me for tea?"
    Hideyoshi, a coarse man, treated his people like children.

He was also pragmatic and admired the Portuguese. After the coup
      that toppled the forty-year reign of Salazar in Portugal,

the victorious faction of his imperial army placed red carnations
      in their gun barrels and made a show of it in green

fatigues before the cameras. My favorite warlord will say in his heart
      what he's known all along—"Flowers transcend

the brute in all men"—though no one shall hear him say this.
      Best to let that pansy Rikyu say it for him.

# PART 3

I was eighteen or nineteen when I pumped gas
on the graveyard shift for Standard Oil
at the company station on 19th Avenue and Irving,
a strange intersection of highway and hamlet.
This was after the Arab oil embargo
when gas was rationed, years before I took
Econ 101 and learned the supply and demand axis
and the word *anomaly*, which I defined for myself.
Pumping gas and washing dishes were not stupid jobs.
Standard Oil supplied me with laundered shirts
shrink-wrapped and pants on hangers, a blue
waist jacket with my name, John, sewn on it.
There are things you can count on as certain
like having your name on your jacket, or Ziggy
Stardust playing "John, I'm Only Dancing."
David Bowie turned sixty today, and whether
you call it "climate change" or "global warming,"
we are in a new era of geography, unfolding
a new cartography of grease: Young Americans
with Chevrolets and Fords, we had a boss
named Johnny Chan at Standard Oil.
I drove a '68 Mustang with a V-8 engine,
black grease caked under my fingernails
and gasoline on my pants that smelled
like fresh paint that never dried.
My friend Duane would die from a gunshot wound
in a crossfire between warring Chinese gangs—
Joe Fong's crew and the Wah Chings.

Duane was at the Golden Dragon restaurant
in Chinatown with his girlfriend, coming from a dance.
By eight a.m. when my shift ended, I had seen the sun creep
up the stunted buildings, the shop doors creaking open,
the *Chronicle* truck dropping off the weekend papers.
I had already heard the dark descanting to the street,
the wail of cop cars crescendo by the time I reached home.
What freedom did I bargain for in sleeplessness?
Was it for pleasure of motion, safe in a car?
Fearlessness I'd long outgrown?
"Let there be commerce between us," Clyde
said to the undertaker in *Bonnie and Clyde.*
My one good thesis in college was that
the Barrow Gang was safest in their cars . . .
Detroit's Big Four was already in trouble.
The exodus from the Motor City began in droves
ten years before my love-in at Standard Oil,
four dozen seasons shy of "Japan bashings"
and the subsequent murder of Vincent Chin
with a baseball bat, before we named such a thing
as hate crime, before the *Exxon Valdez*
struck Bligh Reef in Prince William Sound,
spilling 11 million gallons of crude oil,
a lake of black bigger than the state of Vermont.
Pumping gas in the graveyard shift was
the loneliest job I could find. It was the silence
I bartered for; it was the darkness I knew
the empty highway kept and me illumined
in isolation, catching a glimpse of the ineffable.
David Bowie turned sixty today, and I can see

Alan Lau beginning his shift at eight a.m.
Alan, who was more anomaly than I, shuffled to work
on foot, still a little sleepy. The harbors where
we dock our dreams were continents apart,
but there we were trading shifts at Johnny Chan's
gas station—in league with the invisible.

## ■ DETROIT

My wife carries this city
like a pebble in the heel of her sock.
My mother-in-law with her dour smile
hands me a bean cake from the front seat.
We are driving through Belle Isle.
We come here for holidays and family.
In the hub of the wheel that is the city
hangs a boxer's hand: Joe Louis's giant fist.
Nobody seems to like this thing.
Why, I can't say for sure.
Does it honor a man who behaved well?
Observed all the cardinal rules of Jim Crow?
Malcolm X met Cassius Clay here in 1962
at a luncheonette where the boxer
extended his arm to shake the minister's hand.
Maybe you saw the photo of them in Harlem
in bold and vivid black and white.
Joe Louis, aka the Sepia Slugger,
the Tan Tornado, didn't pay no mind
to young Cassius Clay, even later
after Ali whupped Sonny Liston.
Nobody likes a misbehaving black man
even when he's right. In 1967,
Ali said, "Man, I ain't got no
        quarrel with them Vietcong."

Suspended from the ring, Ali
would come around again. In Belle Isle

trees testify to urban blight, and I am
trying to locate the history of my fear.
The chairs of our dining set are made
from fruitwood trees, chairs
handcrafted in Italy, bequeathed
to us by my mother-in-law
who bought the set from Hudson's.
Tree branches, foliage, roots, and vines—
everything is spreading across America.
Let me honor this woman who hands me
a bean cake and the woman she was
in 1967 giving birth to my wife.
Let me bless this car containing
our picnic through Belle Isle, across
the Detroit River and the long drive
back to where the past is heaped
and folded like an animal asleep
on the soft shoulder of the road.

## ■ THE DISPLACED PERSON

The displaced person comported himself as a dignitary, an ambassador of tarnished connections. If I didn't know better, he was the spitting image of Ben Kingsley's character in the movie *House of Sand and Fog*. Of course he was familiar with the story. "Loved the movie, hated the book," he shrugged. His shaved head and the paisley shawl he wore as a scarf suggested a scholar with a reckless flair. He was gracious throughout the party, making sure he charmed all the ladies despite the presence of his wife, who, dare I say, was guilty of aiding and abetting in how he worked the room. I am certain he loved the movie mostly because of Ben Kingsley. Omar Sharif was the Ben Kingsley of the sixties. *Doctor Zhivago* had played in theaters all of my childhood years in Manila, and Sharif, an Egyptian actor playing a Russian poet in the lead role, played the grief of a displaced person as well as someone like my sentimental mother would have imagined it. In *House of Sand and Fog*, Ben Kingsley had to abandon his sturdy mansion by the sea as well as his high-ranking post only to end up digging ditches by day and doling change as a cashier in a 24-Hour Mart by night. Any immigrant would applaud his resolve. His resilience. That he would come home transformed in a business suit to greet his wife and family in their suite at a high-rise hotel in Nob Hill is about as tragic as our aunties with their counterfeit Louis Vuitton handbags. The displaced person was an Iranian and proud of his origins just like Ben Kingsley's character in the movie. I picture him living in a house with a promontory looking out to the sea and his rooms filled with yellow tulips. Ben Kingsley, who is not an Iranian, but of Indian descent, lives in an old cottage in some quiet village in England. He is a collector of

St. Michael the Archangel in bronzes, paintings, and tapestries, that familiar pose of valor filling walls and tables throughout his home. The displaced person is writing about the life of immigrants where he lives, and for him their stories matter. Immigrants like him with voices cracking in karaoke bars when they sing of their lost homes.

One wintery night, my car gets stuck in the mud.
Atop a long hill, an old couple

inside a blue house. They've been fighting.
I have developed an instinct for such things.

When the husband opens the door,
I am surprised by his gladness

as he hails me as a lost comrade now returned.
They have no telephone, but on their dining table

is a celadon vase bright with yellow tulips,
mid-February in Conway, Massachusetts.

## ■ ELEGY WITH ICE AND A LEAKY FAUCET

He was going to get married in a few days.
The dialectics of fists and ball bats
turned his wedding party into a funeral.
I should tell you something else.
Say like the ice storm in February
or the wedge of lemon in my glass
is as good as any quick fix can offer.
Where I live, you can hear the ice melt. Listen.
Identify ache like degrees of cold,
or say that dull ache can be a color. Pretend it's blue.
Our house is beautiful blanketed in snow.
There is a leak. It is on the plumber's list to fix.
Forget for a moment what's on the list and return
to the drip and the hole to which the leak must go.
Imagine a long drip suspended in time.
This is what I think Vincent Chin saw by the road,
not the leaky faucet of blood that was his head,
not the spring coming with crocuses.
I could have said half a dozen other things
like "war is an abomination"
or "there are wars we can't help fighting."
But you must take a picture. Our house is beautiful
blanketed in snow. It's pretty as a postcard.

# ■ PHOTOGRAPHS WITH IMAGES OF MY FATHER (I–VI)

### I. . . . *As a Good* Babu

He stands there doorman-like below the eaves,
my portly neighbor with his umbrella.
The sky pelts him with rain as he squints
at me stranded on our soggy porch.
My neighbor's a geologist looking for faults,
penciling gneisses, till, and talus.
A happy fat man when it comes to rocks.
Elsewhere, brothers stand side by side, feet
cut off in the photograph. My neighbor's
a bald millionaire larger than Brunei.
Recalling my father's black umbrella,
faithful civil servant, a good *babu*.

## II. . . . *As a Pantoum*

*By day a bamboo cane, by night the sea.*
I give you back the scent of bitter oranges.
You were someone else, if that is possible,
My father younger than I am today.

I give you back the scent of bitter oranges,
Blue cocktail in a tumbler, your other self
My father younger than I am today.
Riddle me this, deep blue sea in your hand.

Blue cocktail in a tumbler, your other self
Unfurling the bamboo mat for your bed.
Riddle me this, deep blue sea in your hand.
Have you forgotten your favorite riddle?

Unfurling the bamboo mat for your bed,
You were someone else, if that is possible.
Have you forgotten your favorite riddle?
*By day a bamboo cane, by night the sea.*

**III.** . . . *As a Sputnik Sweetheart*

I was born, so to speak, under a Soviet natal star.
Mother, with managerial schemes, was a cashier.
Father flashed a badge, a junior Federalli.
A smarmy nest they built for us, then worked all day.
My small delights were my latchkey and color TV.
Got no business pimping my origins, you'd say.
After all, mine's original as a Betty Crocker cake.
Father kept a mistress; common coin for his class.
Ever see your mama catch your papa on the make?
When I moved out, they grew seasick with marital bliss:
Mother manning the stern and steadying the oar,
Father in front of the tube, a pale lit fallen star.

## IV. . . . *As a Lullaby*

How strange the power of recall,
my father remembering 1918
at the Safeway parking lot,
but not the thing he came there for.
Let him remember what is distant
and unimportant, Mindanao
and his father's wounding from the Moro's
blade slicing his left shoulder.
I exhale a cloud of smoke and conjure
my grandfather in his room where anger
was fat as church litanies. A room, blue

of his pajamas and the smell of piss
and Vicks VapoRub. I am that achy stink
of cigar plume that scratches my throat,
coughs that wake me in the middle of night.
Then a snowstorm blew across our town.
Even doctors and nurses were calling in sick.
Vernal equinox's all choked in winter stuff.
My father wades through his complacency,
a living ghost returning to the scene of battle.
Cradled in fog, adrift in suburban lullabies
—that familiar locution for heaven.

## V. . . . *As a Peony*

Here's to the peony in Edna St. Vincent's garden,
the head's repose, too heavy for its shoulders.
Here's to repose whose half sister is Dolor.
Dolor who hates to be called Dolores.
Here's to the song *"De Colores,"*
sung on my father's religious retreat.
Here's to solitude and surrender in order
to cleanse the soul before returning to the body.
Here's to the body that is my mother's lips
kissing my bad old dad bowed like a peony.
Which brings us back to the humble peony
who corresponds in unnecessary
postcards like his first cousin the Lord.

## VI. . . . *On the Fourth of July*

It was a sidelong glance through the fissure,
the errors, the mangled tassel some
mistook for wrought devices I had gathered,
or memories one kept in cigar boxes.
Father, hardly flexing joint or muscle,
managed only a labored turn, turning tight
his neck of crinkled chamois moistened
for car washing and wringing dry—.
Doubtless that tired chorus we sung sounded
dirge-like for Mother's eightieth happy day,
though we dragged the notes with lissome
smiles, hatless heads while cameras snapped
like fireworks in the distance, small puffs of light.

And my mind wandered back to what John Ashbery
once said about Miss Moore, the tricorne-hatted poet
who "gives us the feeling that life is softly exploding
around us." Though around us are only shadows.
There in the arid gray underneath a doorframe,
Father bent as an ampersand in pressed pants and polo,
being and not being, whose steps cancel
each other out just as the traveler's destination
is only one part of the journey, or that the well
is always empty except for the hollow sound
it contains, which is more drink to the soul
than to the parched mouth of my father, whose
pose registers neither salutation nor surprise.

# ■ PROFLIGACY

It was customary for middle-aged men like my uncles to get one.
    The older set went for the clear polish,
my younger cousins preferred the more labor-intensive buffing
    for that fine high shine.
I think the hand & forearm massage matters.
    It should not be perfunctory, but a welcome surprise.
This one woman gazed off in a daydream
    as she made mechanical windmill turns,
clockwise then counterclockwise, with each hand.

Not unlike a firm handshake from someone you meet;
    a limp hand is always cause for unrest.
Maybe because I am a registered Democrat,
    a liberal voter, hence prone to profligacy,
anarchy & softness, she did not want
    to look me in the eye. I mean, *please.*
It was during the era of filmstrips,
    when I was schooled on good hygiene,
affability & occasional grace. *Thunk*, the recording went
    & Sister Mary Joseph turned
the knob of the small projector to get to the next screen.
    Her white hands glowing in the dark
like the plastic Jesus on the dashboard of my mother's car.

# ■ TEA DANCE

My cousin, who never held what you might call
a regular job, strutted to the orders of a different boss.
The one day he took me out for a good time,
we befriended a pair of ladies at a club.
He was a smooth operator, saying just enough
and making the ladies laugh. One had a pretty face,
the other did not, and neither came close to his age.
I was following his lead, but like the women
now at our table, I was just as beguiled
by the courteousness of my cousin
who kept drink and talk in full flow.
The pretty one suggested we head back
to my cousin's place, thinking he was some big shot.
He fluttered his hand, the glint of his pinkie ring
catching the light, his hand waving the way men
do when extinguishing a lit match, and said,
"No can do, girls. The commander is at HQ . . . "
With that the women understood
as if they themselves had to answer to their own chief
who barked out duties and bivouacked with metal,
saluted with starched sleeves sewn with a chevron,
and who took no shit from no one.
No neutral territory was negotiated, and like that
our afternoon of flirting was done.
The ladies made some excuses for departure,
then we both stood up and slightly bowed.
Isn't that what we were trained to do?
"There's no harm in charm," he'd tell me after.

His commander, who welcomed us at the door
when we arrived for dinner, took his face
like a saucer to a cup and paused, then whispered,
"Kiss it." My cousin fired back, "Is that an order, ma'am?"
The moon in its holding pattern was round and bright
as the woman, no stranger to betrayal, sealed her lips on his.

# ■ THE PROVINCES

The chemo made her hair fall,
Smothered her taste for food; her meds—
All colors of the spectrum—tore her guts to shreds.
In her smart skirt, she places a call,

Assumes that all the marginal elements
Of style emanate from a voice in her mouth.
Why is it that longing always draws south,
That the body must respond to its constituents?

To order and name just as the first woman and man
Who roamed the valley of God must have done.
Haunted in the provinces, her ancestral home,

Where sea and clouds are framed by the transom.
Desiccated spirits wallowing in a welter
Of nuisance, their livelihood of *water, no water.*

## ◼ GENERALISSIMO

Behold my great commander,
admiral of marginalia, generalissimo of fog,
boundless note-taker of the sublime.

My older brother maneuvers the iron
steaming along the crease of his shirt sleeve.
"Motion is good," his hymnal line.

Our father's mind and body fled
in pell-mell rout and ruin, and so my brother,
the heir apparent, has assumed

the rank of majordomo to our kin and clan.
Sunday in Ordinary Time, the sermon is on a chapter
in the Book of Kings about Elijah on the lam.

Dozing off, his bloodied body leans against a broom tree.
He wakes to the angel of the Lord, who says, "Rise, Elijah,
and eat this hearth cake and drink from this jug of water."

Elijah, rubbing his eyes and muttering, "Did someone say cake?"
My brother is driving his FedEx truck to collect his cargo.
It is four in the morning and he is wide-awake, alert.

He draws from this clarity; the cleanness of the air,
what light there is, creasing the horizon. He imagines the taste
of metal in his mouth and remembers what will nourish him.

Elijah eats the hearth cake from heaven and walks forty days
and forty nights before arriving in the mountain of God.
Once a cantor for the Legion of Mary, my brother is mute

at Mass, but fluent on the utility of hollow-point bullets.
Today my brother is ironing a basket of work shirts,
digesting this morning's sermon about the prophet Elijah

slaughtering the false prophets of Israel, Elijah on the run
and alone in the desert. My brother, who is quick
to anger and prone to unreason, is like a monk

in his task of ironing; memorizing the highway,
his routes from the south then north of the city,
wrestling with fog at four in the morning,

the steep streets and narrow alleyways at noon,
the great citadels of money, and the cargo he will
deliver with the agency of a bullet's lethal business.

# PART 4

Ebullient as a star-spangled banner
Vallejo's greatcoat was hanging at full mast.
No one, *nadie, nadie,* can see us here
Safe and sequestered in our starched shirts.

Vallejo's greatcoat was hanging at full mast
So impossibly unnoticed.
Safe and sequestered in our starched shirts
Our hairdos with ample wave and hair spray.

So impossibly unnoticed
The broken bric-a-brac tinkling in the air.
Their hairdos with ample wave and hair spray
Ladies with pink purses packing heat.

The broken bric-a-brac tinkling in the air
No one, *nadie, nadie,* can see us here.
Ladies with pink purses packing heat
Ebullient as a star-spangled banner.

Within least-suspecting angles I squat,
               a would be dash if I were punctuation,
a Balinese puppet perfecting its shadow—.

At three in the afternoon my hands began to vanish.
               Kami ay taga-ilog. / *We are from the river.*
When asked where I am from (I have long hair

and my face is shaped like an apple), I answer:
               "I am a ghost in your house, that raft in the distance—,
you know me as your fool whose alias is sufferance."

# ■ A PSALM

Consider the rose, its head bent
    Heavy
        With its fancy of white petals.

The fog that veils an unlit house
    Is drying on the line,
        Fastened by clothespins.

Consider the body that is no longer
    The body,
        The fog dripping on the lawn,

The wind making sails,
    My wife's hands in a pot of clouds,
        Washing rice.

The world is still alive. We will continue.
    Consider the rose bedded
        In the soft folds of fog,

The bowl of rice on the table.

how he lingers in silence, and the interiority of his pause then
sentence writing. "When a country is defeated," Bashō wrote,
"there remain only mountains and rivers, and on a ruined castle
in spring only grasses thrive." Turning his gaze upward, the
moon he keeps to himself the way lovers keep a secret. I love how
in the story that I am reading, Bashō sits down on his hat and
weeps bitterly till he completely loses track of time. In twenty
years I will be seventy; ten years from then I will be dead. Bashō,
who was born into the samurai class, walked in the company of
the thistle. He praised the thistle in his travel sketches. Rivers,
milky stars, the name *Eugene,* the Russian noun for *dance*—or
was that *lake?* When clouds break into stones and strong winds
take the pilgrim's hat, thistledown on his eyebrows and lashes. In
difficult days, Bashō and the thistle sustain themselves with sto-
ries, a cloudburst of stories from their mutual ancestry.

> In riot weather the thistle blooms.
> Love is her economy.

> A lobed skirt of knives
> sings Ethiopic music.

# ■ PANDA WOK GARDEN TAKEOUT

They were three brothers on their way to Shanghai
to trade in their old lives for penguin suits

in a high-flying nightclub of gangsters and cancan girls.
When they finally arrive, they end up as rickshaw drivers.

Like Joey, Dee Dee, and Johnny they were kin
only in a showbiz way. But they live up, of course,

to their dreams in the nightclub industry like the Ramones,
but for a prize as in no-such-thing-as-a-free-lunch prize:

the sweetest one of the three turned to drink, unable to make
the leap from penguin suit to gangster so he drank up the sea.

He drank until whiskey started to seep through his pores,
a pickled herring, pissing off his badass brother

whose major chore was bashing heads. You have to wonder
how in *The Five Chinese Brothers*, the one who drank the sea

managed to keep it all in. Alaska is a wetland now—
and the Bering Sea is but a cup of drinking water.

"When the monsoon season ends the face of the mountain greens and greens." Somehow the repetition "greens and greens" enchanted him. His country is made of desert. One version of Moshe's story told to me by a village elder begins with a common fact: a foreigner wanders up the mountain and is not heard from again. I met a music teacher who told me how he became acquainted with the "daughter of the mountain" the villagers called Maria. Maria is an *engkanto,* a term drawn from the Spanish verb *encantar.* Maria is alluring. She is the first thing that comes to mind when men go missing in the mountain. A music teacher familiar with *engkanto* belief narrates: "While shopping at the mall miles away in Manila, a woman wearing the familiar blue of the salesclerks at Shoe Mart approached me and said, 'Now you can see me in the flesh, not that icy breeze on humid nights, or that lullaby at your piano playing while you slept. As I promised, I would not startle you.'" I asked him if he knew the story of Moshe who bivouacked up the mountain. He acknowledged variations of that theme. One involved a Japanese soldier during the Occupation who disappeared, was found years after the war with a shock of white hair and a rabble of butterflies surrounding him. "He had half-moons in his eyes instead of pupils." The shepherd poet Alberto Caeiro says, "The beauty of nature betrays nature itself since the only true experience is the lived moment." The old people understand what Maria wants. "It is a wedding of dust," one village elder says, emitting consonants of smoke from his pipe.

Think of the bride sipping her
                    miracle wine at Cana.
Think of Maria waiting
                    for the arrival of her groom.

## ■ TREES AS SOLDIERS MARCH

Pity the soul for its rotten luck
For not being plucked ripe from the air.

Whole days spent in cars.
I want to wrap the trees like Christo,

Invent a salve for the illnesses of my affections.
All is silent here. What the fortune-teller

Imparted is enveloped in another language.
How I struggle just to remain upright

When all my unheralded losses pile up
Like a bounty of autumn on the ground.

Is it enough to believe that the colors
Of the Judas tree are beautiful?

That the soul in transit is another name
For apple? Someone should tell me

To go back to where I came from.
Someone should tell on the river

Hoarding all that muck. Everything
Around here is breathtaking, even

If I were a beat-up, broke-ass drunk—.
There are other circles of hell reserved

For other margin-huggers like me
Despite all those statues weeping blood,

Praying their thousand, thousand mighty prayers.
The beauty of my god is allowing me to suffer

While I invoke his name daily through the small
Disasters I make with my own hands.

# ■ PSALM WITH SLEEPING WARLORD

Do you remember the freeway
all gray and curvy like an arthritic elbow?
The green grocer prone to queries
about our nationality. The flat we rented

was a dapper old uncle in a wool frock,
Spreckel's Dairy Factory moored across
the street posed like a decommissioned ship.
The green grocer, a speckled immigrant

now gone, smelled of fresh-cut scallions.
My dad, who read books now and then, said,
"Over the mountains are more mountains,"

a random expression he took comfort in.
Oh, but here you are, my fugitive miscellany,
swaying imperiously in your hammock,
girded with love, sidearm ready.

# NOTES

"Blue Miles": "Here it comes, Grief's beautiful blow job" is from William Matthews's prose poem "The Penalty for Bigamy Is Two Wives."

"Photographs with Images of My Father, VI: On the Fourth of July": "[Marianne Moore] gives us the feeling that life is softly exploding around us," is quoted from an essay by Randall Mann.

"Young Americans": "Let there be commerce between us" is from "A Pact" by Ezra Pound.

"I Envy Bashō's Solitude": "When a country is defeated . . . " is from *The Narrow Road to the Deep North and Other Travel Sketches* by Matsuo Bashō.

# ACKNOWLEDGMENTS

I would like to thank the editors and publishers of the following journals and anthologies in which some of the poems and essays in this collection were first published, sometimes in different versions.

*Asian American Literary Review:* "I Envy Bashō's Solitude,"
    "New Zealand," "Poem in Tagalog," and "Profligacy"

*Cimarron Review:* "The Displaced Person"

*Crab Orchard Review:* "Photographs with Images of My Father, VI:
    On the Fourth of July" (as "On the Fourth of July")

*Dogwood:* "1967" (as "Diane Arbus Prowls Our Street")

*Great River Review:* "Elegy for Ishikawa Goemon" and "Psalm
    with Sleeping Warlord"

*Indiana Review:* "My Favorite Warlord" and "Young Americans"

*Keyhole Magazine:* "Photographs with Images of My Father, IV: As
    a Lullaby" (as "Safeway")

*Lake Effect:* "Water"

*The Louisville Review:* "Cogon" and "Detroit"

*Lyric:* "Allegory of the Laundromat" (as "Laundry List") and "Blue Miles"

*Many Mountains Moving:* "Photographs with Images of My Father, III: As a Sputnik Sweetheart" (as "Sputnik Sweethearts")

*The New Republic:* "Apple"

*The Normal School:* "Monsoon Season" and "Tea Bowl"

*North American Review:* "A Psalm"

*Oxford Magazine:* "The Provinces" and "Psalm with Lathe and Knife" (as "Psalm")

*Ploughshares:* "Trees as Soldiers March"

*Seneca Review:* "Japan"

*Superstition Review:* "Intimacy"

———

"Allegory of the Laundromat," "Apple," "Blue Miles," and "Young Americans" appeared in *Between Water and Song: New Poets for the Twenty-First Century.*

"Here, on Earth" and "Psalm of Myself" (as "Lullaby for Rabbit") appeared in *And Know This Place: Poetry of Indiana.*

"Photographs with Images of My Father, I: As a Good *Babu*" (as "Good *Babu*") and "Photographs with Images of My Father, V: As a Peony" (as "Peony") appeared in *Honoring Fathers: An International Poetry Anthology.*

———

I am grateful to the Anderson Center for Interdisciplinary Studies, Djerassi Resident Artists Program, MacDowell Colony, Millay Colony for the Arts, Ragdale Foundation, and Virginia Center for the Creative Arts for the gift of time, which allowed me to work on these poems; to DePauw University for the Amy M. Braddock Fellowships and the Richard W. Peck Chair in Creative Writing; and to the Great Lakes Colleges Association's Japan Study Program.

I want to thank Sandra Beasley, Debra Kang Dean, Luis Francia, Kristen Lindquist, and Karen Singson for their close attention and generous readings.

**Eugene Gloria** is the author of two previous books of poetry, *Hoodlum Birds* (Penguin, 2006) and *Drivers at the Short-Time Motel* (Penguin, 2000). His awards and honors include a National Poetry Series selection, an Asian American Literary Award, a Poetry Society of America Award, and a Pushcart Prize, as well as fellowships at the MacDowell Colony, the Djerassi Resident Artists Program, and the Virginia Center for Creative Arts.

JOHN ASHBERY
*Selected Poems*
*Self-Portrait in a Convex Mirror*

TED BERRIGAN
*The Sonnets*

LAUREN BERRY
*The Lifting Dress*

JOE BONOMO
*Installations*

PHILIP BOOTH
*Selves*

JULIANNE BUCHSBAUM
*The Apothecary's Heir*

JIM CARROLL
*Fear of Dreaming: The Selected*
*Poems*
*Living at the Movies*
*Void of Course*

ALISON HAWTHORNE DEMING
*Genius Loci*
*Rope*

CARL DENNIS
*Callings*
*New and Selected Poems*
*1974–2004*
*Practical Gods*
*Ranking the Wishes*
*Unknown Friends*

DIANE DI PRIMA
*Loba*

STUART DISCHELL
*Backwards Days*
*Dig Safe*

STEPHEN DOBYNS
*Velocities: New and Selected*
*Poems, 1966–1992*

EDWARD DORN
*Way More West: New and*
*Selected Poems*

ROGER FANNING
*The Middle Ages*

ADAM FOULDS
*The Broken Word*

CARRIE FOUNTAIN
*Burn Lake*

AMY GERSTLER
*Crown of Weeds: Poems*
*Dearest Creature*
*Ghost Girl*
*Medicine*
*Nerve Storm*

EUGENE GLORIA
*Drivers at the Short-Time Motel*
*Hoodlum Birds*
*My Favorite Warlord*

DEBORA GREGER
*Desert Fathers, Uranium*
*Daughters*
*God*
*Men, Women, and*
*Ghosts*
*Western Art*

TERRANCE HAYES
*Hip Logic*
*Lighthead*
*Wind in a Box*

ROBERT HUNTER
*Sentinel and Other Poems*

MARY KARR
*Viper Rum*

WILLIAM KECKLER
*Sanskrit of the Body*

JACK KEROUAC
*Book of Sketches*
*Book of Blues*
*Book of Haikus*

JOANNA KLINK
*Circadian*
*Raptus*

JOANNE KYGER
*As Ever: Selected Poems*

ANN LAUTERBACH
*Hum*
*If in Time: Selected Poems,*
*1975–2000*
*On a Stair*
*Or to Begin Again*

CORINNE LEE
*PYX*

PHILLIS LEVIN
*May Day*
*Mercury*

WILLIAM LOGAN
*Macbeth in Venice*
*Strange Flesh*
*The Whispering Gallery*

ADRIAN MATEJKA
*Mixology*

MICHAEL MCCLURE
*Huge Dreams: San Francisco and*
*Beat Poems*

DAVID MELTZER
*David's Copy: The Selected Poems*
*of David Meltzer*

ROBERT MORGAN
*Terroir*

CAROL MUSKE-DUKES
*An Octave above Thunder*
*Red Trousseau*
*Twin Cities*

ALICE NOTLEY
*Culture of One*
*The Descent of Alette*
*Disobedience*
*In the Pines*
*Mysteries of Small Houses*

LAWRENCE RAAB
*The History of Forgetting*
*Visible Signs: New and*
*Selected Poems*

BARBARA RAS
*The Last Skin*
*One Hidden Stuff*

MICHAEL ROBBINS
*Alien vs. Predator*

PATTIANN ROGERS
*Generations*
*Wayfare*

WILLIAM STOBB
*Absentia*
*Nervous Systems*

TRYFON TOLIDES
*An Almost Pure Empty Walking*

ANNE WALDMAN
*Kill or Cure*
*Manatee/Humanity*
*Structure of the World Compared*
*to a Bubble*

JAMES WELCH
*Riding the Earthboy 40*

PHILIP WHALEN
*Overtime: Selected Poems*

ROBERT WRIGLEY
*Beautiful Country*
*Earthly Meditations: New and*
*Selected Poems*
*Lives of the Animals*
*Reign of Snakes*

MARK YAKICH
*The Importance of Peeling Potatoes*
*in Ukraine*
*Unrelated Individuals Forming*
*a Group Waiting to Cross*

JOHN YAU
*Borrowed Love Poems*
*Paradiso Diaspora*